Ky...

The Inspirational Story of Basketball Superstar Kyrie Irving

Table Of Contents

Introduction

As the title already implies, this is a short book about [The Inspirational Story of Basketball Superstar Kyrie Irving] and how he rose from his life in New Jersey to becoming one of today's leading and most-respected basketball players. In his rise to superstardom, Kyrie has inspired not only the youth, but fans of all ages throughout the world.

This book also portrays the struggles that Kyrie has had to overcome during his early childhood years, his teen years, and up until he became who he is today. A notable source of inspiration is Kyrie's service to the community and his strong connection with the fans of the sport. He continues to serve as a humble, intellectual superstar in a sport that glorifies flashy plays and mega personalities.

Combining superior court vision, incredible footwork, an offensive repertoire that is second to none, and high basketball IQ, Kyrie has shown the ability to completely take over a game. From being a young phenom to becoming one of the greatest guards of his generation, you'll learn here how this man has risen to the ranks of the best basketball players today.

Thanks again for grabbing this book. Hopefully you can take some of the examples and lessons from Kyrie's story and apply them to your own life!

Chapter 1:

Youth & Family Life

The world welcomed Kyrie Andrew Irving on March 23rd, 1992. He was born to father, Drederick, and mother, Elizabeth, in Melbourne, Australia. Kyrie would be the second sibling of three, including an older sister, Asia, and a younger sister, London.

Drederick had a decorated basketball playing career and moved to Australia to play professionally for the Bulleen Boomers. He played his college ball at Boston University. By the age of two, Kyrie and his family moved back to the United States. Because of this, Kyrie possesses dual citizenship in both Australia and the United States.

When Kyrie was four years of age, his mother passed away unexpectedly because of an illness. From that point on, Drederick and Kyrie's aunts would become the main care-takers of Kyrie and his siblings. Upon coming to the United States, the family was located in West Orange, New Jersey. Drederick was still playing adult-league games and Kyrie would become a regular spectator on the sidelines.

In an interview with Nike, Drederick revealed that he knew that his son was special. Young Kyrie learned to dribble the ball when he was only 13 months old. By the time he was four, he could already make baskets using a regulation sized basketball and regulation basketball hoop. By the time he was six, he could already make a lay-up with his left hand.

Drederick, who grew up in a poor family in the projects, wanted his children to have more than what he had. However, he kept them aware of where he grew up and to learn the value of working hard. So, every weekend, Kyrie would spend time in the projects. He said it created a sense of responsibility and humility within him.

Because of the lessons that Drederick would teach his son about life on and off the court, Kyrie was able to develop maturity and wisdom at a young age compared to his peers. He fell in love with the game by watching his father compete and would find his way on the court before long.

However, Drederick did not force Kyrie to follow in his footsteps. Rather, he let his son explore other fields and play other sports. When Kyrie was about 7 years of age, he played baseball against older kids and he excelled in that sport as well.

Kyrie's initial inspiration to play in the National Basketball Association came when he was on a school field trip during the fourth grade. The field trip was to the Continental Airlines Arena, where the New Jersey Nets played their home basketball games. It was at this point that Kyrie implanted in his mind, the dream of playing in the NBA one day.

In an interview during his declaration to join the NBA draft in 2011, Kyrie told the world that when he was ten years old, he wrote on a piece of paper that he would become an NBA player on day. He wrote the word "Promise" and underlined it three times. He hung the note in his locker to remind him of that promise.

Kyrie asked his father to make a basketball hoop in their New Jersey backyard. Since that time, he never stopped playing. His father played with him and coached him. Eventually, he became part of the West Orange Elementary School basketball team.

To help Kyrie improve his dribbling, Drederick wrapped his ball in plastic bags to reduce the bounce. This helped Kyrie focus on his ball-handling technique, which became his foundation for his outstanding crossovers.

By the time he was a teenager, Kyrie was able to use his natural athleticism and learned skill-set from his father to become one of the better local players in his age group. He would go on to play for the Road Runners in the Amateur Athletic Union (AAU) circuit.

Throughout his childhood years, Kyrie was encouraged and supported by his father. When he was in 8th grade, he told his father that he wanted to be the best point guard in the state of New Jersey. His father told him that he should work for it - and so he did! Kyrie started playing six hours a day and developed the skill-set he learned from his father.

Kyrie, when asked how his father influenced his career, answered that Drederick laid the blueprint and the steps for him. It was up to him what he wanted to do with it. Kyrie said that when the two of them watched games together, he would tell his dad that he could do the same moves. Drederick would tell him that he could certainly to it.

Till this day, Kyrie is thankful for his father for always bringing him to his games and teaching him how to be a man. In his interview during the Draft, Kyrie thanked his father for being the best coach and the greatest critic he had.

Chapter 2:

High School

Kyrie would go on to attend Montclair Kimberly Academy for his freshman and sophomore years of high school. He became a member of the basketball team and wore jersey #11. He showed promise early on, as he posted averages of almost 27 points and 10 assists, to go along with 5 rebounds and 4 steals per game.

Kyrie was known to play on both ends of the court, dominating on both defense and offense. He was almost unstoppable on offense, as he could finish spectacularly under the hoop and was also deadly from deep. He became known as one of the best, if not the best, jump shooters in the league. He was also a dreaded clutch player because he could knock down buzzer beaters, even with three players guarding him.

With the lessons instilled in him by his father, Kyrie never forgot that he was part of the team. He did not only score points, but also distributed the ball and created plays for his teammates. Kyrie was steadily working on achieving his dream of becoming the best point guard in the state of New Jersey.

His efforts for his freshman season would make him the school's second player to ever score 1,000 points in a season. Seeing that he was still a freshman at the time, Kyrie had a bright future ahead of him.

He would continue this momentum into his sophomore year, when he was able to lead Montclair Kimberly Academy to a New Jersey state title. He showed clear dominance in his prep league and there was quite a buzz among the locals in the area.

Because of his transcendent talent, Kyrie and his family decided that he would be best served to transfer to St. Patrick High School for the final two years of his high school career.

St. Patrick's competition would provide a bigger challenge for Kyrie, as well as provide him with more visibility to collegiate and professional basketball scouts. Not only was the competition at a higher level, but the teammates Kyrie played with would also be better than at Montclair Kimberly Academy. He would play alongside hot prospect, Michael Kidd-Gilchrist, one of the highest ranked players in the nation for the class of 2011.

Shortly thereafter, Kyrie became part of the St. Patrick basketball team and donned jersey #24. After having to sit out for the first 30 games of the season because of the rules regarding high school transfers, Kyrie was able to make his presence felt as soon as he stepped on the court.

In Kyrie's first season with the team, he would go on to post averages of 17 points, 5 rebounds, 6 assists, and 2 steals per game. More importantly, he, along with Michael Kidd-Gilchrist, were able to lead the team to the New Jersey Tournament of Champions title. This would be the school's third title in four years, showing that they were a powerhouse in New Jersey basketball. It was also during this season that Kyrie got his first in-game dunk.

During his middle school and high school years, Kyrie trained with Coach Sandy Pyonin of the New Jersey Road Runners (NJRR). He went on to play in the National Amateur Athletic Union (AAU) Championships with NJRR, wearing jersey #4. He led the team to the festival championship and won the MVP title in the process.

Kyrie and Drederick would often play one-on-one after the latter pointed out Kyrie's tendencies. Growing up, Kyrie had never beaten his dad. But when he was sixteen, Kyrie finally beat his dad by a score of 15-0. Drederick swore that he worked hard defending his son, but his son had finally surpassed him. According to Kyrie, it was a moment that boosted his confidence. He finally beat the best player he had ever played against, who knew all of his best and worst moves, and was his greatest critic.

The father and son would still play against each other from time to time. Drederick, however, admits that he can no longer be competitive with his son. So, playing with Kyrie just became his best cardio workout.

Because of the spectacular play in his junior season, Kyrie was invited to play at the Nike Global Challenge in August of 2009. He would go on to be named the MVP of the tournament, as he led the USA East team to a championship victory. His averages in the tournament include over 21 points and 4 assists per game.

Kyrie started his senior season with a personal goal he set with his father. He wanted to finish his high school career as the number 1 ranked player in the country. He trained very hard outside of school, continued his training with the Road Runners, and studied film often. His efforts paved the way for an explosive senior season in 2010.

However, an unexpected ban came from New Jersey basketball officials, when it was concluded that St. Patrick High School had violated a rule regarding practices being held prior to the beginning of the sports season. The ban would make St. Patrick ineligible to play in the state tournament. Despite such a blow to the program, Kyrie and his teammates would still play at an extremely high level during the regular season.

The team would post a 24-3 record and was able to win the Union County Tournament championship. Personally, Kyrie scored 24 points per game, while dishing out 7 assists and grabbing 5 rebounds per game. Because of this impressive season, Kyrie became nationally regarded as one of the best players in the entire class of 2010.

He was even ranked as the number two basketball player in the entire class by Scout.com. Rivals had him listed as the fourth highest prospect, and ESPN listed him third. No matter the ranking, it was obvious that Kyrie had the potential to make his dream of playing NBA basketball become a reality.

After his senior season was finished, Kyrie was chosen to play for the 2010 Junior National Select Team. He would later be selected to play in the 2010 McDonald's All American Game, as well as the Jordan Brand Classic. These honors would allow Kyrie the opportunity to play with other elite high school prospects from around the country and see where he stacked up.

Impressively, he was able to take home Co-MVP honors in the Jordan Game, along with Harrison Barnes. Before his college career, Kyrie also able to win a gold medal at the FIBA Americas Under-18 Championship.

According to Kyrie, though he dreamed of being an NBA player for many years, he only truly believed that he could become one during his senior year. He was convinced that he would make it to the prestigious league when he noticed the progress of his game and how it stacked up against other elite talent.

"Be hungry, and be humble." This was the maxim Drederick taught Kyrie during his youth. Kyrie said that he painted the maxim on his duffle bags to remind him to keep his feet on the ground, as he was beginning to reach national and global acclaim as a hot prospect.

Enjoying the national spotlight during his junior year, people treated him differently and would stop to ask for his autograph. The locals would treat him like a celebrity. However, Kyrie made it a point not to allow the fame into his head, by constantly thinking about the maxim.

Kyrie said in an interview that he liked that he was being noticed, but he did not pay attention to it. So, he continued to live his last year and a half in St. Patrick as a regular student. He participated in other sports and school activities. He even bagged one of the lead roles in their school's adaptation of Disney's High School Musical. Despite attending basketball practices, he attended the school play practices faithfully. He nailed the high notes of his song and perfected the dances.

In a local school interview, Kyrie was quoted as saying that he wanted to show the world that he had more talents than just basketball.

As a high school student, Kyrie did not only set goals for basketball. He also set goals in his studies. He was determined not to get any grade of C's. It was not acceptable for him. He took pride in achieving high grades, along with his good basketball skills. Thus, he was constantly working - in and out of the court.

Over the years, Kyrie did not lose his love for music. He learned to play the saxophone, baritone, and trumpets.

Chapter 3:

College

In the first half of his high school senior season, Kyrie committed to play basketball for Duke University on a televised ESPN-U broadcast. As one of the highest ranked players in the world, Kyrie's decision to attend Duke would provide hope amongst the Blue Devil's fanbase, as well as add to Kyrie's rapidly growing resume.

Perhaps most importantly, Kyrie would be able to learn under legendary coach Mike Krzyzewski, who was the head coach of the historic basketball program at Duke.

Kyrie joined the Blue Devils and assumed the lead point guard position from the start. By the end of his first eight regular season games with the team, Kyrie was already making a case for the NCAA Freshman of the Year award. He had compiled averages of over 17 points, 5 assists, 4 rebounds, and 1.5 steals per game. Furthermore, his shooting percentage was impressive for a point guard, at over 53 percent from the field.

However, an unexpected injury occurred in the ninth game of the season, when Kyrie would severely injure a ligament in his right big toe. It was concluded by team doctors and coaches that Kyrie would need to undergo surgery. The surgery would sideline him indefinitely and he began the rehabilitation process shortly thereafter.

Luckily, the Blue Devils were able to keep it together long enough to make the NCAA Tournament and Kyrie worked hard to make it back for the first game. Kyrie's announcement to return for the tournament brought a rejuvenated energy to the team.

After wins in the first two rounds of the tournament, Duke would eventually lose in the Sweet Sixteen to the University of Arizona. Kyrie scored 28 points in the game, but it would not be enough to overcome a well-coached, talent-filled Arizona Wildcats team.

Upon season's end, Kyrie announced that he was going to declare for the 2011 NBA Draft. Personally, Kyrie promised his father that he would finish his college education at Duke University, before going to the NBA. But, after experiencing the reality of a serious injury, as well as the fact that he had performed well in the tournament, Kyrie arrived at his decision to go pro. He believed that he would be best served to leverage the momentum built and skills learned during his time at Duke, into an opportunity to realize his childhood dream.

Kyrie, in an interview, said that he still wanted to keep his promise to his father. He promised to finish his college education, even if it might take a little longer than the five years he promised after high school.

Despite his early departure from the Blue Devils, Kyrie continued his relationship with Hall of Fame Coach, Mike Kryzyzewski, which he fondly calls Coach K. Kyrie said that Coach K continued to be his mentor and encouraged him to get back on his feet, after he missed his first NBA Finals in 2015.

Chapter 4:

Professional Life

After he declared his intention to be drafted into the NBA, Kyrie went back to training. Drederick was behind him all the time. He encouraged his son to work harder than ever before.

So, every time Kyrie stepped in the gym for training and practice, he worked harder, until the day of the Draft. And that training certainly paid off, as NBA teams started showing more interest in him, especially the Cleveland Cavaliers.

First Season (2011-2012)

Kyrie would be one of the most talked about prospects heading into draft day. Despite his immense talent and mature personality, many teams around the league felt that he could be injury prone and did not possess an imposing build for the professional ranks. However, the Cleveland Cavaliers, who had the first overall pick, were very interested in drafting the 6' 3" Blue Devil's point guard to become their point guard of the future.

The team would choose him as the first pick in the entire draft and Kyrie would sign a contract shortly afterwards. Upon joining the team, Kyrie chose the jersey number 2. During the Draft, he promised his father that he would be ready for the team every single day, and he proved it when his rookie season began.

Kyrie began his NBA career as the starting point guard. He would join fellow rookie, Tristan Thompson, on a roster that was in rebuilding mode from the year before. The Cavaliers had a great deal of work cut out for them, as they were one of the worst teams in the Eastern Conference during the previous season.

Kyrie would not disappoint Cavalier management, as he performed up to standards in his rookie season. Along with teammate Tristan Thompson, Kyrie was chosen to participate in the Rising Stars Challenge during the 2012 All-Star Weekend. He played for team Chuck and played wearing jersey number 23.

He would go on to score 34 points in the Rookie-Sophomore Game and even take home MVP honors. The performance put Kyrie on the national radar as one of the best young players in the Eastern Conference and gave casual fans a look at what he was capable of - as he went 6-6 from behind the arc. He also gained popularity due to his sick crossover moves, pull-up jumpers, and three-pointers that many would say were ridiculous. Because of this, he was given the monicker "Kyriediculous".

Kyrie would keep the momentum going post-All-Star Break, as he finished the season winning NBA Rookie of the Year honors, receiving a total of 117 out of a possible 120 first-place votes. Not surprisingly, he was also named to the NBA All-Rookie First Team as a unanimous selection.

His season averages of over 18 points, 5 assists and 40 percent shooting from three point rage, showed that Kyrie had the potential to become a franchise player for the Cavaliers in the future.

However, although Kyrie was able to post incredible first-year statistics, the team did not improve much from their previous season. The roster was still in rebuilding mode and they were in search of steady leadership and coaching.

In the lock-out shortened season of 66 games, the team was only able to win a total of 21 games. They ranked 13th among the teams in the Eastern Conference.

Second Season (2012-2013)

Kyrie's second season with the Cavaliers started off with an obstacle, as he suffered an unfortunate injury to his index finger while playing a pre-season game against the Dallas Mavericks.

Kyrie was injured from slapping his hand on a padded wall after committing a critical turnover. The injury required surgery and it kept Kyrie out for the next three weeks. He watched his team struggle to win games from the sideline.

However, he would soon return to score a career-high of 41 points against the New York Knicks. In doing so, Kyrie became the youngest player in NBA history to score 40 points in Madison Square Garden, since Michael Jordan accomplished the feat in 1985.

By mid-season, Kyrie was selected by coaches around the league to participate in his first All-Star game as a member of the Eastern Conference All-Star team. He would play well in the game - scoring 15 points, dishing out 4 assists, and grabbing 3 boards.

Additionally, Kyrie was chosen to play in the Rising Stars Challenge once again, this time as a second-year player. He would have another great scoring outing, putting up 32 points for Team Shaq. Lastly, Kyrie was also chosen to participate in the NBA Three-Point Shootout, where he would go on to earn 23 points in the final round, enough to win the event.

By season's end, Kyrie's sophomore campaign showed statistics of almost 23 points, 6 assists, and 4 rebounds per game. He was becoming one of the best young point guards in the league heading into the off-season and the future looked bright for his career. The squad showed some improvements in team chemistry and ball-movement, but were still unable to crack the playoffs in the Eastern Conference and remained 13th in the ranking.

Third Season (2013-2014)

In Kyrie's third season, he was chosen by the fans to be the starting point guard for the Eastern Conference All-Star team. Kyrie was becoming a fan-favorite around the league, in large part because of his flashy crossovers, incredible shooting range, and the ability to make plays for others off the dribble.

Furthermore, his ability to finish at the rim as a point guard, was already being ranked as one of the best in the league, along with San Antonio Spurs' Tony Parker and Oklahoma City Thunders' Russell Westbrook.

He would go on to take home All-Star Game MVP honors due to an impactful game with 31 points and 14 assists. Kyrie continued his excellence into the second half of the season and even posted his first career triple double in a victory against the Utah Jazz.

Later on in the season, Kyrie scored a career high of 44 points against the Charlotte Bobcats. His consistent play during his third season would give him averages of almost 21 points, 6 assists, and 4 rebounds per game.

The Cavaliers ended the season with a significant jump from 13th to 10th. After the season ended, Cavaliers' management rewarded Kyrie with a $90 million contract extension that would span the next five years.

Not only was it obvious that Kyrie had the ability to be a franchise leading player, but he was also developing into a better overall leader and floor general on the court.

Fourth Season (2014-2015)

Before the end of the 2013-2014 season, there were rumors that LeBron James was coming back to play for the Cleveland Cavaliers. There were also rumors that Kevin Love, another franchise player, requested a trade from the Minnesota Timberwolves to the Cavaliers. These rumors created the hype of the formation of the "Big Three" or the James-Irving-Love connection.

But prior to that, there were questions about what Kyrie would become for the team. When he was drafted by the Cavaliers four years prior, team management wanted him to be their new franchise player after LeBron left for Miami. In essence, Kyrie was given control as the undisputed head of the snake. For the previous three seasons, the Cavaliers were, categorically, Kyrie's team.

Then, the rumor of Kevin Love's inclusion to the team added to the suspicion that the Cavaliers could be setting Kyrie aside. Some feared that there would arise some power-grabbing issues among the three stars. But Cavaliers' management was quick to answer any potential media stir-up.

A day after Kyrie signed his $90 million contract extension, LeBron finally announced that he was going to sign with the Cavaliers. Shortly afterwards, news was confirmed that Kevin Love was traded to the Cavaliers for rookie Andrew Wiggins and second year player Anthony Bennett.

Thereafter, management revealed their original plan of acquiring the other two star players. It was to create their own "Big Three", who they believed would bring them their first championship. Management hoped that their Big Three would be comparable to the Celtics Big Three, which included Kevin Garnett, Paul Pierce, and Ray Allen. The Boston Celtics also won a championship after their team was formed.

During the first few games after the formation of the team, the Cavaliers suffered losing streaks. Soon, they got back on track. They finished the season as the top team in the Central Division and ranked second in the Eastern Conference, behind the Atlanta Hawks. It was a big leap from 10th in the previous season.

Kyrie averaged 21.7 points, 1.5 steals, 6.1 assists and 3.6 rebounds per game during the regular season. In an overtime game against the San Antonio Spurs, Kyrie scored 57 points, breaking the previous Cavaliers franchise record of 56 points, set by his teammate LeBron James in 2005. It was also the first time that a player scored more than 50 points against the Spurs, while being coached by one of the legendary coaches, Gregg Popovich.

As the season progressed, Kyrie and his teammates showed the world that the Cavaliers were not a one man show. While Kyrie called LeBron the best player in the world, he felt more than ready to carry the team on nights that LeBron was struggling. The two players started playing like a wrestling tag team, each stepping up when the other seemed to be needing help.

Kyrie played the first playoff game of his career against the Boston Celtics on April 19th, 2015. The Cavaliers won the first round, despite losing Kevin Love to a season ending injury during the series. Then, they moved on to win the second round against the Chicago Bulls. They followed it up with a sweep of the Atlanta Hawks for the Eastern Conference title. However, Kyrie missed the last two games of the Conference Finals because of a knee injury.

He came back to play his first NBA Finals game against the Golden State Warriors. But, during overtime, he suffered another knee injury and had to leave the game. He was consequently declared to be out for the rest of the Finals. The Cavaliers lost to the Warriors in six games, despite an all-time great and valiant performance by LeBron.

Kyrie's playoff averages were 19 points, 1.3 steals, 3.8 assists, and 3.6 rebounds per game. Many experts and retired players regarded this as a great performance for his first playoff showing. Many also predicted that he would come back the next season and would become a more special player for his team and the NBA - thanks to this tremendous experience.

Fifth Season (2015-2016)

Because of the knee injury he suffered deep into the Playoffs, Kyrie had to sit the first two months of his fifth season. He returned to play on December 20th, 2015. The James-Irving-Love connection was really rounding into form during the season, and the team finished first in the Central Division and the Eastern Conference. Kyrie finished the regular season with an average of 19.6 points, 1.1 steals, 4.7 assists, and 3 rebounds per game.

The Cavaliers were looking dominant in the first two rounds of the Playoffs, as they swept the Detroit Pistons and Atlanta Hawks rather handily. In the Eastern Conference Finals, they faced the Toronto Raptors. The Raptors managed to delay the Cavaliers' march into the NBA Finals by stretching the series to six games.

Once again, the Cavaliers matched up with the defending champions Golden State Warriors. Kyrie struggled to find a rhythm during the first game. Though he totaled 26 points, he only made 7 out of his 22 field goal attempts.

The team lost the first two games in devastating fashion, but were able to bounce back and win the third. By the end of Game 4, with the series heading back to Golden State, the Cavaliers were down 3-1.

From that moment on, Kyrie and LeBron put the team on their backs in an attempt to make history. No team had ever come back from a 3-1 deficit in the NBA Finals before.

In Game 5, the duo put up 41 points each - forcing a Game 6 back in Cleveland. It was the first time in the history of the NBA Finals that two players from the same team would score more than 40 points each, and win the game.

Kyrie would also become one of only two players to score more than 40 points in a game while converting 70% of his field goal attempts. The other player was the legendary Wilt Chamberlain.

Kyrie and LeBron continued their magic and won Game 6. In Game 7, Kyrie helped his team make history by hitting a game-clinching pull-up three pointer in the final two minutes of regulation. While Kyrie may not have won the Finals MVP, his performance in the totality of the seven games was one of the greatest that the league had ever seen.

In most any other year, Kyrie's stat line and impact would have garnered the award for certain. However, LeBron led all players on both teams in every major statistical category (points, rebounds, assists, blocks, and steals), showing that he was still the best player in the NBA and one of the greatest athletes and basketball players to ever play.

The Cavaliers' championship victory was also the first major league sports championship the state of Cleveland had ever experienced in 52 years.

Chapter 5

National Team Career

Kyrie was offered to be part of the Australian National Basketball Team that would represent Australia in the 2012 Summer Olympics. Because of his dual citizenship, he was eligible to play for the Australian team. However, he turned down the offer and chose to play for the USA National Team instead.

In 2014, he became part of Team USA and represented the country in the FIBA World Cup. He was the only Cavaliers player on the team. He was reunited with his Blue Devils Head Coach Mike Krzyzewski.

Team USA won the FIBA World Cup and Kyrie was named the Most Valuable Player of the tournament. His success with Team USA led him to be named the 2014 USA Basketball Male Athlete of the Year.

Kyrie's stat line for the 2014 FIBA World Cup: 12.1 points and 3.6 assists per game. He scored a game-high 26 points in the final round against Serbia.

Many players who represented the US in the FIBA World Cup opted not to represent the team for the 2016 Rio Olympics. Some claimed that their management would not allow them, while others were afraid of contracting the Zyka Virus.

Whatever the reasons, Kyrie decided to continue his commitment to the team. He joined Team USA and went on to represent the country to the 2016 Rio Olympics.

He would again make history by being Team USA's youngest starting point guard, since the Dream Team was created in 1992. Kyrie won a gold medal after USA defeated Serbia in the final round once again.

Chapter 6:

Personal Adult Life

Trivia

Kyrie is certainly one of the most unique superstars that we have in the National Basketball Association. Not only is he clearly intelligent and well-spoken, but he has a fun side as well. He enjoys singing, dancing, and even playing the baritone saxophone - clearly possessing an aptitude for music.

Kyrie has also stated that he enjoys reading in his free time and keeps a personal journal as well. If he can find time, he is very interested in enrolling in voice lessons and piano lessons as well.

When asked what he would have become if he was not an NBA player, Kyrie said that he could have been a musician. But his father believes that he would have become a sports journalist or a sports newscaster because of his love for writing and his confidence in speaking.

An interesting aside about Kyrie, is that his godfather is former NBA star player, Rod Strickland. Rod and Kyrie's father, Drederick, were friends when Kyrie was young and they have maintained a close relationship over the years, even as Kyrie has developed into a star in his own right.

Rod Strickland, being an endorser of Nike, made sure that his godson had his own Nike shoes since he was a baby. Kyrie eventually signed with the sportswear giant in 2011.

Kyrie is regarded as one of the rare players to have mastered the backboard angles. When he was asked about his secret, he revealed that it was because the hoop in the family's driveway was bent. Instead of getting it fixed, he learned to work with his angles.

One of the scariest times in Kyrie's life was when he was ten years old. It was during the 9/11 terrorist attack. Drederick used to work in the Twin Towers, but three weeks before the attack, he changed jobs and worked in a different building near the tower.

When the Twin Towers collapsed, parents rushed to the schools to be with their children. Drederick could not come for Kyrie and his sister. Kyrie was very worried. It took six hours before they finally received news that his father was safe.

Endorsements and Business Venture

Kyrie has become well-known for his commercials with Pepsi Max. In the advertisements, Kyrie takes on the persona of "Uncle Drew", an older man who routinely shows up the youngsters in pick-up basketball games. There have been multiple episodes in this series of commercials.

In addition to working with Pepsi Max, Kyrie has also had a few other television appearances, including on the Disney XD series, *Kickin' It*. Kyrie was also the cover athlete for the video game, *NBA Live '14*.

In 2011, Kyrie signed with Nike, during his rookie season with the NBA. As a child, Kyrie dreamt that he would have his own signature shoes and would use it to play in the NBA

Christmas Day game. By 2014, he became one of the 20 athletes who had their own Nike signature shoes. His shoes were called the "Kyrie1".

He first used the shoes on December 25th, 2014 when the Cavaliers played the Miami Heat during the NBA Christmas Day game. The "Kyrie1" was followed by two more. The "Kyrie2" was launched in 2015, while the "Kyrie3" was launched in June 2016, weeks after the Cavaliers won the championship.

Kyrie became the new face of PSD underwear in 2015. His job was not limited to modeling the product, but he was also given the authority to design his line of underwear. He was also assigned to be one of the trend spotters for the company.

In 2016, Kyrie was offered an endorsement contract by Skullcandy. The agreement included an equity stake in the company and the authority to make creative inputs in the company's product. He is also allowed to create and promote his own line of headphones.

According to Kyrie, the Skullcandy deal will help him achieve his dream of creating something which reflects his true creativity, taste, and style. The deal may make Kyrie a trendsetter and a business mogul.

Chapter 7:

Philanthropic/Charitable Acts

Even though Kyrie has only been a professional athlete for a few years, he has already developed a close relationship with the community of Cleveland. His charitable acts include helping young boys and girls to develop a passion for reading and learning.

Through the Cavaliers' youth programs, Kyrie spends time reading to children and encouraging them to focus on education as a main pillar in their lives.

Kyrie is an active member of Best Buddies, a non-profit organization that helps people who suffer from intellectual and developmental disabilities. Best Buddies encourages and helps to facilitate one-on-one friendships between people. He became a member of Best Buddies even before he became a member of the Cavaliers.

Kyrie first became a best buddy for "Jacob". When he attended the Draft in 2011, Kyrie made sure to wear his Best Buddy pen, in order to make people aware of the organization. Soon, he became a global ambassador for the organization.

When asked why he maintained his volunteer relationship with Best Buddies, Kyrie answered that he loved how the organization promotes friendship among humans, regardless of their circumstance. In September 2016, Kyrie plans to establish the first Kyrie Irving Basketball Challenge in Cleveland, Ohio to raise funds for Best Buddies.

In 2012, in cooperation with NBA Cares, Kyrie chose UNICEF to be his principal charity while in the NBA. Consequently, in 2013, he went to a three-day trip to Africa, in cooperation with UNICEF. He visited schools under the UNICEF Schools for Africa project, and was joined by former NBA Player and African native, Dikembe Mutombo. Kyrie participated in educational programs and events, and even danced with the students.

When asked about his experience, Kyrie mentioned that he was fascinated by how the kids wanted to learn and how eager teachers wanted to teach. He also said that he understood how early education was important and how instilling sports at that early stage can make a big difference in life. In December 2015, Kyrie reportedly donated $30,000 to UNICEF USA, through the Elvis Duran Show.

Despite leaving as a toddler, Kyrie still has some connection to Australia and has made it a point to give back over there as well. He helped to fulfill a fund-raising event in Albert Park, Australia that was run by "Helping Hoops". Helping Hoops is a charity organization based in Australia which runs weekly basketball programs for the youth.

Through the efforts of the charity, over a thousand disabled and disadvantaged children are impacted each year. Kyrie helped raise more than $15,000 for the event and even put on an incredible display of shooting, as he hit 108 out of 118 free throw attempts - all in the span of five minutes.

In 2016, Kyrie joined ProCamps and hosted the two-day Kyrie Irving Basketball ProCamp. During the event, Kyrie eagerly joined and supervised the events. He made sure that each child would get his autographed souvenir and would be taught well.

He concluded his ProCamps event by giving 190 pairs of shoes to the Boys and Girl's Club in

Cleveland, Ohio. The 190 pairs represented the total points he scored during the NBA Finals against the Golden State Warriors.

Aside from participating in NBA Cares projects, Kyrie often joins other charity events hosted by his fellow NBA teammates and peers.

Chapter 8:

Legacy, Potential & Inspiration

Even though Kyrie is still very young in terms of his profession, he has already begun to develop a legacy. After LeBron James left the Cleveland Cavaliers for the Miami Heat in the summer of 2010, the franchise turned to Kyrie Irving a year later in hopes that he would be able to help turn the team around.

After experiencing their worst season in over eight years, the Cavaliers were counting on Kyrie to provide a much-needed spark. In his few short years in the league, Kyrie has already shown that he is one of the best ball-handlers in the game.

His ability to make defenders fall asleep and then blow by them is second to none. Furthermore, his change of pace dribble allows him to break the defense down on the fast break as well as in the half court set.

One of the most impressive aspects of Kyrie's game is his ability to hit clutch shots. The Cavaliers have begun to count on Kyrie to get them a basket in close ball games that are determined by a possession or two. Even if he does not shoot the ball himself, he is able to make plays for his teammates by getting into the teeth of the defense and setting them up with the ball in their desired position.

He can shoot the three point shot with ease, whether it be off the dribble or in a catch and shoot scenario. His range is as good as it gets and he is not afraid to use it. His confidence from thirty feet away is what keeps defenders on edge and forces them to play him honestly.

Maybe what is most impressive about Kyrie's game is the fact that he is not physically imposing or exceptionally explosive. While he still has great agility and foot-speed, he is not as physically gifted as players like Russell Westbrook and Derrick Rose. However, he is arguably just as, if not more, dangerous offensively, mostly because of his mastery of the technical skills of the game.

He is able to make shots over seven footers in the paint, not by dunking over them, but by using his crafty floaters, finger rolls, and scoop shots. These abilities make him similar to players like Tony Parker, in that he can get a shot off in a multitude of ways and seems to get into the paint with ease, despite usually being one of the smallest players on the court - a true testament to the hard work that he has put in over the years.

Kyrie certainly has the potential to become one of the best scoring guards that the game has ever seen. He has already set a number of impressive records and has an All-Star MVP award, showing that he can compete against the best in the league and float to the top.

Conclusion

Hopefully this book was able to help you gain inspiration from the life of Kyrie Irving, one of the best players currently playing in the National Basketball Association.

The rise and fall of a star is often the cause for much wonder. But most stars have an expiration date. In basketball, once a star player reaches his mid- to late-thirties, it is often time to contemplate retirement. What will be left in people's minds about that fading star? In Kyrie's case, people will remember how he led a franchise in their journey towards a championship.

He will be remembered as the guy who plucked his franchise from obscurity, helped them build their image, and honed his own image along the way. He will also be known as one of the guys who made the 2016 NBA Championship Title possible for the Cavaliers after a 52 year drought.

Kyrie has also inspired so many people because he is the star who never fails to connect with fans and give back to the less fortunate. Noted for his ability to impose his will on any game, he is a joy to watch on the basketball court. Last but not least, he's remarkable for remaining simple and firm with his principles in spite of his immense popularity.

Hopefully you've learned some great things about Kyrie in this book and are able to apply some of the lessons that you've learned to your own life! Good luck in your journey!

Made in the USA
Middletown, DE
31 March 2017